And I am Terrified

Chris Baterna

BookLeaf Publishing

Presentation by *BookLeaf Publishing*

Web: www.bookleafpub.com

E-mail: info@bookleafpub.com

ISBN: 9789357211819

First edition 2023

DEDICATION

To my micro-manager, Chad,

who held me accountable for every. single. step of this (and also designed this very cool cover):

Get some sleep.

To anyone, who realises that one of these poems is about you:

I hope it's not one of the sad ones.

ACKNOWLEDGEMENT

Most of the people, who I would like to acknowledge for the creation of this collection, are not alive - nor in any way familiar with me. I tip my hat to them in the poem, 'Lunch with Great Bearded Men', for simply being great minds that shape the world I live in.

Those, who inspired me and ARE alive, I doubt (with hope) that they would ever read this. But in case they do:

One of my professors at the University of Sydney, Dr Ben Brown,
taught me for every Ancient History unit I ever studied, successfully converting me from a Modern to Ancient (specifically Greek) History student. Ben was my first introduction into the greater world of critical thinking, philosophy, sociology, and historiography. Every valuable life lesson I've retained from a class has been in one of his tutorials, and the struggling conflict of these are very evident - not just in these poems, but in my wider identity approach to life. Ben

also probably went way too easy on me, when uni got hard. Thanks, Ben.

My family and friends, who had no idea I was even working on this, thank you for serving great inspiration for both my poetry, and my many thoughts. There's a poem for each of my family members - not just out of obligation. Thank you for your patience and tolerance. Particularly, I take inspiration from my parents - two selfless Filipino immigrants, whose sacrifice in building their three kids' lives in a completely new country: I am just starting to realise with age. A lot of identity crises come with being a child of immigrants, so I can't image how tough it is to be them. But my parents made their family turn out pretty good.

I'd also like to thank the very few friends, who did know (some extent) of this project, and who willingly read and critiqued some poems. Leila, Gaz, Jonah, and Julia, who actually read/heard a poem or two: it means a lot.

Finally, the one person who knew, and held me accountable for the entire process of this, was my great friend, Chad. For someone who doesn't know how to read, you did an exceptional job helping me render and refine my work. All the late nights you spent micro-managing me on calls, I swear I will make up to you. You are the craziest, most hardworking friend I know, and I could not be more honoured to have your support in my work (and artwork on my cover).

PREFACE

Honestly, I thought I would have started with a novel.
Many of my friends and mentors have for a long time pushed me to write some grander narrative, and I know I would enjoy it. While I could have hidden my impending thoughts under an elaborate mask of a novel, it would not have been so honest.
Seeing now, how 21 days of poetry can push my creative boundaries, I am glad I chose this route.

The questions I ask throughout this collection revolve around my disillusionment with the world, against my originally underdeveloped idealisms about morality, love, religion, and existence. I delved into various critical '*ism*'s and was particularly drawn to the mess of the human condition and culture as explored by Foucault and Post-Structuralism. Through historiography and literary criticism, which tainted each text I consumed (often unintentionally, and without welcome), I came to the conclusion quite adamantly: The world is so, so messy, and we will never truly know each other because of it.
I was only able to gain insight and comfort into these conflicts, from the study of philosophical works and global literature -

including those of spiritual/religious nature unfamiliar to me. And although disheartening at first, human-ness explored by the likes of Dazai, Shelley, Poe - and anyone who created the AMC series, 'Mad Men', generated the needed curiosity to appreciate the world's complexity. Previously, I was only exposed to what my dear parents (who had the best intentions for me) and very-Catholic alma mater (a more complicated question) had taught me; I urge everyone - no matter the state of your beliefs or religion, to explore another. Explore how other people understand the world *without* any presuppositions of superiority. Read doctrines, discuss ideas with its followers, or simply have a good chat with your incredibly wise acupuncturist – never limit your existence and understanding of the world to what you've been given. Truly dive into the places you fear the most - for me, this was a world without the God I grew up knowing and fearing. Whether, at the end of the struggle, you hold your faith or not, your resolve in the outcome will be more justified. My studies of Buddhist thought worked in almost perfect conversation with these philosophical revelations. That is, not to say that I am now Buddhist (or that I have rejected Catholicism all together), but that there is infinite value in learning and appreciating other belief systems and cultures. I found the messiness of the world - the 'Terror' of the unfamiliar - to be directly interconnected to the things that make the world wonderful.

The poems of the first half (up to 'Shaun Street') view this Terror with a stubborn hold on my idealisms. Like most people, I fought against fear and had no intention of embracing it. The latter half, however, touches on Terror with more curiosity, appreciation, and understanding of its place in life. Fear indicates something more valuable than perfection: something more human.

'Of Faith and Fathers', introduces the many questions I had, when I first embarked on my critical theorist journey. It depicts a very intense 'shake-angry-fist-at-God' moment, which I'm sure none of my religious family or friends would be quite pleased with... But its questions are honest.
I hope, with all I can, that every person may be understood in their situatedness. And if the God of my parents is truly so understanding, I'd hope there is compassion for my anger too. This religious fear is recalled in the final poem, 'Reaching For the Fruit', but in far less isolation. By the end of the work, I come to view human nature as still quite ugly and full of Terror; but there is nothing for which I would substitute it.
In the same way, my fears of moral ambiguity and cultural subjectivity is presented quite drastically in 'Caligula'. It is mirrored with

more appreciation for our complexity of philosophical range in the penultimate, 'Lunch with Great Bearded Men'. The Fear I come to appreciate in each aspect is culminated, still with some anger, but mainly with a mindful pride in humanity's ugliness. Loss and regret are not just explored in the sense of one's death ('The Moth') or the fear of losing a friendship ('My Dear Friend, How Are You?') – but in the regrets of a surrendered life to situation ('Beware the Housewife'), isolation ('In Fragility'), numbness ('Shaun Street'), and to a mind-numbing job ('Paper Shop Prison'). These truly terrified me, so that even the joyful poems in hope ('Hotaru no Hikari') and indulgent memory ('The Homecoming Ritual') depict Fear as something to be fought against.

But Terror is born from wonder. We start vulnerable and overwhelmed ('Station Street'), and learn to live with Fear as a friend, reminding us of precious moments ('Ghosts Feign Affection', and 'Noodles'). We can only appreciate the leaps we make for our ambitions, because of the Fear holding us throughout the process ('Satellite Stars'), and that we have allowed it to guide us gently in everyday life ('Above Some Ramen Shop'). Terror makes value in each new experience ('A Toast to the Stranger'), and fighting for ambitions ('Rage, O Street Musician'), and perhaps – sometimes, even romantic pursuits ('Recently, Roses').

I will continue to embrace Terror – not in the hopes of losing it, but in careful listening to what it wishes me to find.
So now, the only thing I will have to truly, negatively fear is the way friends will ask me why there are only 20 poems for a work of 21 days.

Of Faith and Fathers

I stare down my fleeting youth enshrined.
What am I to do with this beating life of mine?
It rages through my lungs;
It begs for new kindling - to feast,
But I am rendered silent...

I am well acquainted with the moon and stars,
with coffee and cards,
with the silent spirit breaking,
when a broken love falls hard.
But still I search...

At the threshold of New Age, we circle back to start.
To what useless use of youth should I dedicate my heart?
We search for God in poetry,
in scattered moments - broken lines;
but if He too searches for me,
then God, why do You hide?

Does He hide from my restless shame,
as I pick at bone and skin,
and rip my soul in halves
to a light they call a sin?

I have seen the people's faith,
for I have never been so blind
to their love and hope and terror
- their remorse for lack of mine.
They've left their homes in search for You;
their bloodied brothers, a fear of others,
and angry vultures
flew in.
But my father never left me
to his lonely guilt or dreams unbuilt;
to fight alone
in ruins.

Does God truly watch my father's head,
bowed to his working desk?
then bowed in prayer on Sunday,
then bowed each night in rest?
And always for freedom, always salvation,
always family, always love.
Always sacrifice, and dutied diligence, always calling,
reaching, searching in mumbles.

And yet,
I am terrified.

Has God ever felt pure terror?
To lose all that He is -
To lose us?

Or is He so ready to strip His child
of ink and skies
and coffee cups?
Yes, my father with his human heart
hopes for my human best.
In his human eyes of ignorance,
my life is no mere test.

And so I search for meaning -
For whoever is keeping score;
if He is here for all of time,
what am I in it for?

Father, keep praying.
Though I cannot promise
that when I bow with you to the altar, it is God
that I am praising;
For your imperfection shines far more deeper
to me.
My trust is in the terror
of the weak and broken man;
Forgive me for this trespass,
But dad, only if you can.

For I am terrified of many things
of God, and good and evil -
But not of you.

The Homecoming Ritual

Sister, hold my hand as we climb the steps to our front door,
soaked in the tired whispers of the school day done.
Today, sun does not greet us in her afternoon glow;
Today, the sky pours down to reach you -
a blanket embracing us in varnish,
to seal these few steps in the lacquered liquid of memory.

Lay the umbrella to rest against the humble grey of brick.
Mumble for my patience, tell me to be quick.
Tell me to shake the mud from my shoes;
Groan as I refuse,
and splash in my puddled youth.
Be the sacred conductor to secret chorus of clicks and unlock
sacred removal of bag, and blazer shirt and sock.

Sister, look! I move so quickly, tell me to be slower;
Tell me to take

my time…

Why do I hurry?
You should have told me sooner.
Now, tell me sooner.

But look how fast I run!
I can't check to see you watch;
Kindly indulge me with your attention,
and I'll kindly refrain from begging.
Why do you move so slowly?
What secrets do you find in these dripping
walls? Tell me.

Sister, sister, watch me watch the TV
and I will wash out your voice;
when you fix things - far more broken
than my little plastic toys.
Tell me to tell you of homework undone.
Tell me in voices that voice you as mum.
And I'll protest to hear these same words
repeated,
by mum; by dad; and you again.

I'll drown this truth out with static cartoon,
as you drown the day from your lunch box;
Argue with me…
as I reach for a spoon…
to eat the lunch,

I left in mine.
Sister…
Tell me that it's rotten.
So I can tell you that it's fine.

Argue with me now, until I want to scream;
for I am terrified of the day you're suddenly sixteen,
and I will hate you for simply being sixteen;
Your work and wisdom won't make sense to me by then;
but I'd continue playing hero,
and cast you as villain.

So, Sister, lock the doors.
Don't let Time's tears leak in;
Sit still with me – don't listen
to the twisted fateful grin
of retrospect.

Sit.
Please.
Here.
Watch the cartoon.
Or hide in your room.
We'll think this scene of afternoon could be completed with a song.
But neither of us know how to turn the music on.

So, for now, sit.

Hear the refrigerator hum,
Hear the static, feel the carpet,
Watch the windows.
Wait for mum.
The little lights on potted plants
are sleeping by the door.
Shall we mimic plants before the spring?
Shall we, too, sleep on floor?
But then the phone will ring.
And we wait for mum once more.

Then you follow her instructions.
I will follow you around,
as you wash the rice and roll your eyes,
when I make the smallest sound.
Soak in this sacred rhythm, while it grows
with us
under a beating that draws closer.

Rain watches us and pauses by our front
steps.

It notes the umbrella we left out to dry;
for mum to note it briefly;
for dad to walk right by.
It chuckles at our childish attempt of ritual.
--at my childish attempt to rhyme.

The light outside is dim, but it bears down on me.
It blows the static in my eyes
until you are smudged,
and I promise I'm reaching out to fix it.
But each line I draw fogs the glass more violently,
until here I stand before
only a mirror

But sister,
I think I see you
a little clearer.

蛍の光 (Firefly Light) - Haiku and Tanka

蛍から
小さな光
世界まで

If only faintly,
If only small and for me,
Your firefly light:
It shines for hope of my own
For when I am terrified.

My Dear Friend, How Are You?

My Dearest Friend,

Is it a rite of passage to watch you slip away
from my stubborn grip,
and stand as my pillars of youth lose their
shape,
blurred into a wall?
Am I to wait and watch it slip?
Must I let it go?
Who knew there would come a day,
when our friendship would hang by the
carefully threaded bow,
existing simply because we want it?

We'd sworn secrets and promises
that retrospect taints with a thought:
That 'they were half-made, and loosely
bound.'
But I hope in our blissful youth,
we made them with every intention to be
fulfilled.
Over flowerbeds and sandy coasts,
from yours to mine, and the school yard,

stories flowing from youthful tears
to the giggle of wine-stained teeth:
We raise a glass to each one of them.

But who are we now?
Is our trusted hold – our grip on hope
strangling us?
Are these roads too travelled, that we unravel
at the wheel,
too trusting in the passage home,
we pass each sign to stay awake?

When we sit with indulged ears
to the stereo man singing sadly,
of a love slipping away,
a defeated tune, sighing, of course it ends this
way…
He sings in dragging metre,
for he knows the song will end.
And so must his love. And so must this time.
He is aware of fading melody, so sweet to me
--and still,
He drags on and shrouds himself in sweet,
melodic prison.
We know the song will end.
And yet we sit and listen.

My friend,
I see you sway in time.

I fear you'll sway too much and miss the rising harmony;
It is our own. Do you notice?
Or are you so far from me?
My friend, please don't sing the melody.

These days, far from the coast and flowerbeds,
I watch among the crowd.
I am captivated by your sweeping growth,
still traced of the footprints we left behind,
But reaching further now.
You shine, my friend, so brightly.
There is no disturbance in between us
for bitterness to cast her shadow from your light.
Keep this in mind, while I dwell on crowded thoughts,
never so quiet as crowds need be.

Though I am terrified of the days
when we know not what to say;
when I creak rusted, asking you,
not of fear, but of "what's new?"
When the roads run down your shoulder,
and you ask directions home.

I am not so terrified of my thoughts now.
But that terrifies me more.

That our threaded time of stitching
was a string attached and torn.
Just a bow, just a moment,
just the hole in the wall of your newly
furnished room:
Still there when we don't see it.
A quiet smile, discovered only
in your monthly dust and broom.

I stay because you've stayed before.
I cheer, though I am drowned
by the crowd's roaring praise,
a war and maze
of dues unpaid and paying.

We cheer on because we say we must,
We sort and brush off
mistrust of each other
in hopes to uncover the times
our timely hopes aligned.

And I will stand here forever, my friend.
For the sake of threaded bow
If just for its beauty and memory.
If just for the detail of a footnote.
If just to be captured in this instance,
till the end of this poem,
for my hopeful grasping of time,
if you find me again

in tears, or if you still shine
just as brightly
to complete this…

Beware the Housewife

Beware the housewife, lurking in silhouette,
caressing your desires through window light,
calling temptation upon drink and hearth,
born in sun's rest: daughters of night.
Watching from the door, down the porch
steps,
offering comfort in her time and her tea.
Beware your own thoughts in desire for it:
The siren singing in sweet melody.

For she waits in each waking morning.
She stands still at the kitchen sink.
Eyes in search of a wanderer,
mind with much time to think.
Beware as you approach her front door.
Beware as you sit down to talk.
Note her good smile and good greeting,
Note the third time you're meeting.

Beware the housewife missing her child
spoon-feeding her dreams for your own.
Pulling new colours from your world outside,
to paint herself mirror of home.
Still your heart and carefully listen
for her secrets wrapped neatly in cloth

through wide pearly smiles and pretty house songs.
Search not for what is, but what's lost.

Beware how you feel, when you ask how she does.
Beware if she blinks at the question;
Because she is wife to husband and house,
such nonsense should never be mentioned.
If she makes mess - of her own spilling thoughts,
they are hers alone to clean up.
For pretty housewife in her perfect life
could not possibly feel herself stuck.

Notice her house: how much of her is there?
Where are her thoughts neatly piled?
Where does she keep her forty years lived?
In which mirror does she practice her smiles?
Beware the lonely housewife, who's been ripped from her past
and whose husband is never at home.
She helps her good neighbours wash stains from good shirts,
but deals with his laundry alone.

Truth of her wisdom may slip from her cup;
Beware your brief capture of glimpse,

For she'll sweep it away, stacked under the plates,
thrown out, quickly hidden, and rinsed.

But who listens to her scrambling eggs each morning,
for her child scrambling out the door?
Her friends once flew by on the hour hand,
but fly to her street no more.
Who listens to her when she, after twelve cups,
shares memory of carefree years?
And instantly insists you share tenfold,
as she scrambles and hides a loose tear?

Beware the housewife who's travelled the earth,
but now exists solely at home.
For she has lived some infinite worlds,
and you have just lived your own.
I give you warning to beware the housewife,
for you are far weaker than she,
who tidies cruel truths I am terrified of,
then spares you her time and her tea.

Caligula

When he walked the treaded coast in boast of
who he was,
and sought watch of the ocean in tremble,
Deemed weak by fellow man, though no
fellow saw unmanned:
the tortures that the emperor resembled.

Why did he fight the sea? Poseidon --
Neptune, as he knew.
Was it watching in its wash, so proud?
Fellow man may roar louder than the scream
of Neptune's power,
to weigh on the laurel and shroud.

What makes man fight the ocean? What
makes him hate his own,
if not the same thorns budding love?
Man's sadness in fellow's absence, or
madness struck upon him,
From some act of divinity above.

Then Caligula was trapped truly, in chains of
his own vessels:
The emperor – an error of nature.

History laughs fondly peering down at sanded man,
in glass towers of morals far greater.

We pull mad man's face through time and in tide,
'til he is hero, singing recklessly bold:
"A horse! A horse! My fellow man for a horse!"
No ocean is so easily dissolved.

Will you have me stab glass towers in him - Caligula's sin;
Cut roots of madness in motion?
But I am terrified, to wake one day in pride,
as I march fellow man to the ocean.

In Fragility

I sit here alone with three versions of me,
In my cold nakedness,
stirring in my condition.
It is heavy.
And I, human - as they long to be,
am fragile: in body, too,
But more-so in the mind that asks,
"Am I fragile?"
"Can I carry this?"

And the hopes of answers feign friendship.
They seduce me in a grin.
But I have studied lies in lung-full's
to know when truth is thin.
And truth is thinnest in this room,
in my mind of coward dreams.
Of selfish ruins at my end,
traced back to selfish means.

But am I truly so terrible? One part of me mumbles,
Slowly unwrapping the smoother skin of the palm.
One side: rough, familiar
One side left unharmed.

I dream of reaching exhaustion
at the end of my life,
For my hands, studied, to pull at one's mouth,
praising:
"You were loved."
I dream for the skin on my hands to peel off,
so the imprints of another remained
- forever showing that I had held these other
hands,
and they gripped on back, just as tightly.

Truly, Two parts of me agree,
Love exists and is weighed in infinite forms.
I dream of learning another.
"But," says the other,
I am terrified of never knowing my own,
that memory, at my end,
would not bless me with the reach of one
more.

So I dilute these hopes to fiction:
to poetry, in compromise
to say that I have somehow achieved them,
tasted and seen them.
But my hands will forever be cold,
and silently reaching for contact.

"Is it selfish for want of return?"

Truly, I try to be selfless,
Truly, I try less to yearn.
But three parts of me are human,
and often, in my isolation and ignorance, I
hope.

And it traps me, for love is not Love
with the intention:
within which I do seek reflection.

But why do you worry for a selfish world?
Do you wish to be above, or within it?
How will you hold love? Can you hold love?
If you were created from Love,
Why do you beg for more?

But, you are so in love with the world, you
leak with it.
Perhaps, if truly crafted by Her, She filled you
so surely
- but in Her own generous wild,
left you with incomplete seams:
cursed and lucky to wander the world
in search of someone to stitch you.

The Moth - Sonnet in Iambic Pentameter

Flown in - a flash into my frightened eyes
The wretch-ed and the fo-ul creat're mock'd
My lungs pound loud to heartbeat paralysed
An unforeseen terror with whispered knock.
Why does it haunt me in the dead of night?
What warnings does it scream from
palm-sized wing?
That I, in indecision, am made blind
To all the truly terrifying things.
Have you been watching me from mem'ry's
wall?
Or waited for my flight to you each night?
The image of you waiting haunts my fall.
You wait and only I am terrified.

Cries Envy to the brave who watched you fly,
But me, forever holding my Goodbye.

Paper Shop Prison

There is nothing Romantic about this scene,
but I am violently devout.
I work my soul for the clock
and hearsay numbers adding up.

I wait, and watch, and sit
on my ambitions;
superstitions on my daily toil and stitch
me up and then I'm breaking
again and over again;
thinking a million miles a minute
to a million better plans,
where my aching bones aren't wasted
but here I stand.
Here I stand.

Watching my routine as my shadow slips
darker,
and crawls on the floor for me to suck into a
vacuum;
along with it: dust, and figures, and questions
I mumble.
When? How? Why?

My youth betrayed from dreams of vitality;

My daily surrender to the scanning beeps,
and computer clicks, beep, and paper stacks,
clack.
Add a heaviness of question,
dragging along my feet:
Am I a wasted talent? Is talent waste on me?

And my betrayed youth questions also
-- screams to me, "Get out!"
My resolve shamefully crumbles
and yet, I am devout…

I spit angry words when I am terrified.
I spit at pride and hopeless hopes,
throwing matches on clinking spirits,
drowning dreams in fire.
My vision from this distance saw a funeral
pyre.
but as I walked among the ashes
I see they were no threat;
Merely candles hoping to be passage-
Wasted now.

But this image only laughs,
when I'm pulled back onto shore
for it was no coast at all;
I just work in a fucking store.

But even still,

I'll beg to see resonance between me and the
shelf
thinking some greeting card could comfort
myself,
and sing:

When we're chosen,
for a moment,
we will burn ourselves bright;
Even to surrender
our paper fragile nature,
for a service and hope we might
not be tossed away with such immediacy
Forgotten, when comes the night...

I'll hum my wallowing sadness against the
whirring of machine,
My throat seems to be the only part of me
unstuck.
I'll drown in thoughts until someone comes to
charm or anger me,
stare down my fleeting youth on the card that
reads, "Good Luck!"

Shaun St.

In my weakness I return here,
as soldier marches to heated rest –
as sun and body fall heavier,
so I find my gravity calling.
Heavy thoughts meet heavy end,
at the stretch of land around street bend.

I took the train home,
to stretch my soul;
but time like worried mother
ushers race from my legs.
The sun sleeps on my furrowed brow;
May I rest out here for now?

So I stretch my fingers through the dirt
in search for you.
My throat turned desert for two streets down,
my feet dig deep into dirt as protest;
shoulders slump off the day's toil,
Hopeless, planted in soil.

So wash me in my thoughts,
drain me, winded path,
hold me by this edge,
for I am truly breaking,

Stitched in mere pretences
Abandoned by kiss of senses.

Subtle breeze, haunt me.
Sing your lonesome through my veins.
May I feel my skin to know:
my lungs indeed fill with you.
Don't let the sky melt into something colder
before I feel much older.

Night watches the breaking.
Hunt continues two feet down,
for signs of life echoing any part of me.
Yearning to be Frankenstein's son.
Witness my daily descent.
Yearning for terror again.

Station St.

From my weakness I was reborn:
A sailor in old months' lighting.
The moon rises in fragility,
still bound in her gravity,
and offers hand in starry lend,
for heavy thoughts now start to end.

I take the bus home tonight.
A single seat in humming,
Glassy eyes through glass and skies,
smudged dark to make out one thing:
That I was here in memory;
That I was rested and did beat.

And I recall my search for you,
though you were right where I had left:
in cold teal room, with soft teal chairs.
Hung on paintings, practiced breath.
As I rock forward on jolting ride,
your promised stay echoed in mind.

"I will not leave you - I swear it.
If even you hit against the wall,"
A floodgate echoes through the room,
out the door, down the hall.

Ears singing, washed in melody again.
Erupted tears, old faithful friends.

Neon lights softly descend,
woken by new signs of life.
Gently round this dim, dipped bend,
concrete shines in rainy night.
I see footprint where I have stood:
pressed deep in pain, but it is good.

Fragile child sat on metal beams,
wonder-gazed at each passer-by,
Helpless, crying quiet tears
and still I know not why.
But my very worst no longer hides:
Brave and breathing, terrified.

Ghosts Feign Affection

I am terrified of the ghost in the old school gym,
when the afternoon sun sheds on floors;
making even the day's dust echo angelic –
as if they, too, breath our rest.
as the pounding heart resists all but this moment,
knowing this hall does not mark where you stood,
but the very existence of it
calling through ghosts,
as if it hosts the epitome of your childhood.

We are terrified of the convincing conviction
the ghosts play on strings of heart,
when we believe
even shoe squeaks
against the floor are some kind of music
finer than tune of your choosing.
There is great terror in how easily we melt
towards the whispers of such fiends,
painting a heaviness attached to the scene,
as if you did indeed love this place –
as if it hold no ill memory.

How convincing they are, to draw tears from terror.

The terror erupts like a newborn,
screaming protection from all else,
screaming to be held preciously,
as precious things are.
Be it sure love, or thawing nostalgia,
there is terror, hand-in-hand.
The terror in losing this moment to its own existence.

But terror is warm, like the first summer in aged reminiscing.
It howls for her children: "Affection!"
to cherish inevitable forward motion of train,
or streets in rain,
the call of your name, and namely moments
at the brink of insanity,
and where you climbed from there.

To know terror is to know Love
and Her powerful ghosts –
But to know also that they are enveloped
only by such fragile things,
Like the sun on the gymnasium floor.

Satellite Stars

Tilting left, under soft suburban skies,
craned towards the netted window.
Calling whisper reaches into my lungs,
from further lands, where fresher winds do
blow.
It lifts my chest, ever so slightly,
I am inclined under moonlight's softest
embrace,
She whimpers – as if in sadness,
though the tide chases her in coasts far away.

How brave you were, brother, to start
dreaming at three,
as I learnt watching two steps behind you.
One wonders the wishes you must have
counted
to walk yourself surely in each change of
shoes.
Did you dream from this window each night?
Were your whispers, too, carried by breeze?
Or did dripping candle provide greater light,
for you to be greater dreamer than me?

I mirrored your posture, fumbling often in
reach.

Your bones stretched, so I pulled at my own.
And when distance stretched too, in time and in face,
still I studied your footprints at home.
Though further now, I still recall your pose,
My brother, you've gotten quite tall,
And your purpose shines proudly on your blazer pocket:
The same light from when we were small.

When others will look from your old bedroom window,
they may point to the stars in the sky,
to dampen your victory in luck and in wishes,
blessing Artemis in ritual pride.
But I lie here now, brother, and see them:
The stars that you wished upon
were satellites, made by the human.
But your sweated dreams were not wrong.

So watch me strive for my own, my good brother,
Do you see I can walk with some pride?
Do you see I am terrified less wholly now,
when I lie here and still often cry?
I try not to fall under this night's rosé daze.
Though captured in watch, I keep stars at a distance,

But, cool linen to touch offers sweeter dreams;
I am child, soon plunged into starry-night visions.

Above Some Ramen Shop

When he's showered golden in soft orange sky,
lying in crumples - arm shading his eyes,
When his singlet blends cotton in the bed where he lies,
He'll know he is at peace.

When he stretches his neck to his left – to his room,
or glances right - out the window to soak in the view
of the quiet side street in the late afternoon,
He'll feel it is a dream.

When his eyes circle round with the old ceiling fan,
slept luxury bothered by no particular plan,
after work, run, now resting in Sendai, Japan,
He'll measure his ends from his means.

When the sizzling downstairs wafts up to his floor,
His chef-neighbour knocking with food at his door,
in a silent-smile deal for restaurant chores,

He'll melt into casual scene.

When the thermostat hums in changing of seasons,
or doors open wider to let humble breeze in,
When life becomes habit without counting reasons,
His visions will be truly complete.

This is the life his youth built upon.
These are the sore bones that stretch proud and strong.
This breeze from his dreams is familiar song:
He wrote it when sounds did not sing.

Although it is little, this life is his own.
Although not made golden, it is carefully sewn.
Not from billboards or suits, nor quick-fallen Rome;
it is firefly light that rings.

He prays for the habit when painting is dried,
no longer urging to Romanticise,
Allowing himself to be terrified,
and truly be part of the picture.

When he's forgotten the rules of his youthful arrival,

When life becomes more than a game of survival,
Romance fades slowly, he reverts to his primal,
His little life made all the richer.

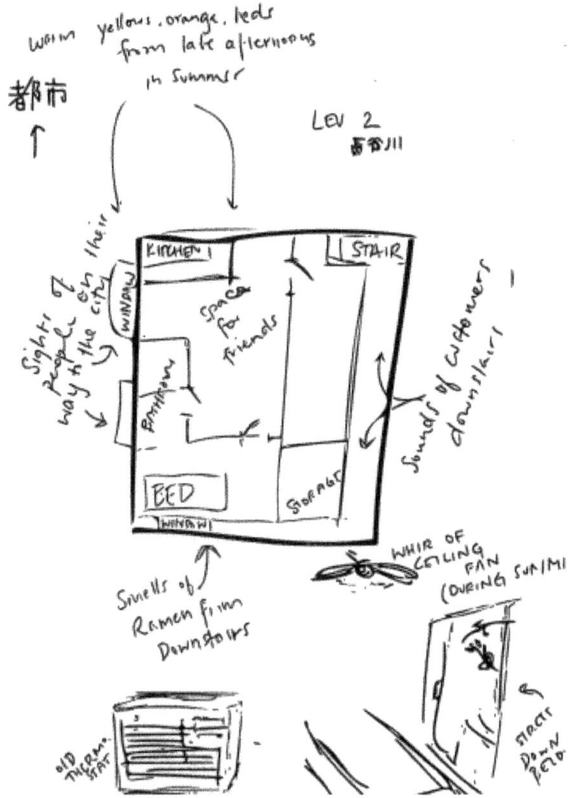

Noodles

My mother holds a tradition,
I deemed as superstition:
of eating noodles on each birthday.
For a long, happy life,
she'd summon fork and knife,
to prepare the noodles
- Her way.

Perhaps I believed,
for a momentary scene,
that some magic worked in each bite:
An honorary task,
like the clinking of glass,
to a future, or past, just as bright.

But years and cravings fill us.
We watch ourselves to the seams.
We watch our fill, and who we are,
and I am terrified of what it means.

In each birthday dinner,
the noodles got thinner;
New traditions brewed quietly in time,
But still, each New Year wish
was a small side-plate dish:

Noodles, spring onion, and lime.

Now my sister prefers pasta;
I still prefer rice;
Brother cooks
his own meals these days,
and dad stops craving at night.

Wander rinsed dry,
in longer bones - opened eyes,
until they were noodles and nothing more.
And mum knew that I knew,
and I knew she knew too,
but still she'd stack plates, keeping score.

In brief happenstance,
while performing this dance
of pulling the pans from the shelf,
I almost did miss it,
under noodles in rinses,
a whisper, as if to herself.
In long, winding noodle,
it slipped from her mouth,
and tradition was twisted in fork:

"It's my parents' favourite," she said,
dipping her head
to the bowl of string, tangled cords.

Tangled here: affection and love,
steam reaching above,
and it burnt my senses,
learning her goal:

Here is my mother,
in prayer with another,
Whom I had only met in bowls.

In this instant, suddenly,
this taste made sense to me:
If who we are is what we eat,
then my mouth has been wasted in rhymes;
hiding my face, my country - my taste;
Hiding Pancit under lime.

A Toast to the Stranger

The swirling crowd of Friday rush:
crash to touch, bustling and blushing faces all
flushed,
What chaos must
they stumble towards?
It's been a week. Weakness with time,
wilting resolve, problems unsolved,
and what is this rhyme?
Cursing crowds dispersing, and still they are
swirling
Pedestrian streets seem shrinking, then
turning –

But you…
You breathe from the side alley.
The choking charge of afternoon,
quietened to its end,
in your tired, open arms:
A breath.
To notice body aches, and pains
and cloud lines slightly speaking
of silent leaking rain.

Slumped from Main Street, you are welcomed,
stray weary wanderer.

The smell of rice from secret peace –
a hole in brick travelling deeper.
Traces of city rush do spill softly inside
but from garlic, onion, smoky sweet sizzle,
your craving cannot hide.

You sit in place at the lonely man's bar.
Prying at the frying pan, from front row
seating,
tossed in trusted sizzle, loudened by the
drizzle
of the downpour outside, beating.

You marvel at the chef, quietly until
another lonely stranger –
strangely closer than your thoughts
comments first.
Then a burst
of laughter and onslaught
of running conversation – with no meaning or
depth.
Just meaningless exchange of meaningless
breath.

"From abroad." – she says.
"From out west." – then you, "all my life."
"That's nice. I came here for the view."
A laugh at the glances of rain now unsealed.
A nod in agreement:

"I'm here for a meal."

You share this quiet noise with this quiet
stranger:
Share a meal, share some cups,
and some jokes that bring laughter
- Nothing at all that a week will remember.
Stories you tell that months' time soon loses,
but perhaps you might --
in slip of mind, down the line,
when you glance at a view,
wonder if her stories ever reached a
conclusion.
And though you may be terrified
To reduce a being to a night.
Dance in your honesty: Raise a glass to honest
pride.

Steep in the moment, away from familiar
friends,
to whose lives you've dedicated yours,
Breathe in each aroma,
silly question, and loose secrets outpoured.
It needs no rhythm, or purpose, or rhyme.
But every so often: a thought that it might.

When the meal is done, the light and rain
retreat,
Tap the counter, knowing

you may never again meet,
But that this time was warm – as was the meal.

Bid her, "good luck".
Thank the chef with, "goodnight."
Re-emerge to the street,
right back into life.

Recently, Roses

Recently roses have appeared in my life,
almost everywhere I choose to see them.
Each one – bloomed and budding, capture my
eyes
in petal nets of red and white.
I see them in every garden and vase.
I see them in every tree and bouquet,
I see them in every book and colour,
in every path home, and each poem prayed.

Perhaps it is coincidence.
Perhaps it is a choice.
To see these roses everywhere,
in scent, in taste, in voice.

But retracing the roses, it is no coincidence:
they point to two years back.
Among past swamplands and deserts,
where they shouldn't have bloomed.
Among my new isolation,
When I met you.

It is no coincidence,
that with each shade of purple,
the very first thought belongs to you.

No Divine Intervention plants the roses I mind.
It is simply intentions sung true.

It does not pain me to know
that the rose, when exposed,
fades quickly come the winter;
I know thou art more temperate
than rose -- too tender, yet
it grows in hopes to mirror you.
And I'll watch it grow regardless.
For these feelings to me are new.

If ever you were to doubt this truth,
I would slowly graze my fingertips across your every thorn.
so when my scarlet meets you,
I may compare its muted colour:
casting even a shadow, freeing
the deepest glow of any being.

But if you were to tell me it was no rose at all,
lend me your patience,
as I search to give you another blossom's call;
a flower by other name,
But never fear the tearing of stem,
I will adore you all the same.

I am terrified only of grasping too tightly,

that you would, in your terror, cut through
me.
But even this fear is but shadow,
gone when all else abandons.

So tell me when I hold too closely,
Tell me if you'd rather leave
me to my memory.
I swear it's enough to see,
that we once did
rest in this garden.
Let me recall,
as my final pardon,
that I wrote of roses
in your apartment.

- After Roses -

I can recall two years at the store,
We're on the street,
We're by the lights,
We are Everywhere,
and Nowhere,
when where wasn't the matter.
I can recall laughter.

I recall laughter and whispers and nervous
breaths,
and the silence in knowing:

to not care if I am not glowing
the same way you do now,
to not care if
my truth is showing,
or if a hair strays,
or hours on my wrist.
How could I care,
when we're laughing like this?

Rage, O Street Musician

Rage – oh Muse, sing of it,
on this stage of rush and concrete,
Roar your voice through the street,
Sing your own Odyssey.
Summon your wrath
like Achilles.

You have lived centuries; Millenniums
conquered –
and rarely changed is your name.
Though the samurai now dresses as Wall
Street broker,
You are messenger all the same.
But now in your summons, I dare not attempt
to rhyme,
for your turning and tuning is far sweeter in
sound,
than any scaffold of words I could throw
together.

Blessings on the house and the world you
build tonight:
an oasis feeding every moment with a purity
of its own.
Immersing every wanderer with a choral rain,

Though briefly, I am terrified of this fragile moment
breaking under streetlight and jealous noise,
You, craftsman gently fold:
every conversation, quiet engine, rolling motion
of the city spilling orchestra in your art.

Play your power, oh Muse, when you are passed by,
and when the city lights steep the night in green glass.
For even those stumbling and mumbling
through your rough winded stage,
are guided to you by Dionysus.
And the sober ones, friend - we hear you.

We hear your life start at seven a.m.
to the sounds of corporate ladder clique.
We hear the bed sigh with the dreams that it keeps,
when the verse is stuck in its chord,
and you wait for dawn chorus again.
We know you are destined for greater than now,
more than the street, more than the stage,
more than the stadium lights.
You are for Olympus, for Heaven, for mind and for peace,

A legacy we'll pull until it is close enough
for you to seduce through wandering alley.

So play, oh Muse. Wake from your bed.
Demand the gods' full attention.
If their eyes wonder past you in search for
Orpheus,
Rage that they have wronged you also.
Rage at the power you have, overfilled,
that they give you no place to erupt.
Meet their eyes - look not for Eurydice.
Charge in full tempo through your hubris.
Until Homer wakes from his slumber,
and your legacy raises his brow.

Lunch with Great Bearded Men

I sit for lunch with great bearded men.
My welcome is uncertain, but I sit to hear
them talk.
Some cheap form of Homer summons the
room.
"Friends, pull your seats.
For today, we discuss what we must:

How shall the world turn?"

Aristotle glances at Buddha.
Christ breaks his bread passed around.
Marx and Rizal pull their notes out,
And Dazai lies drunk on the ground.
Behind him, on chairs, some Writers do write,
from countries and times, spread of my
interest.

Though they do not all have beards,
Though not ALL sit at the table,
They are well able, to have others hear:
Their thoughts, their questions,
their drunk murmured lessons,

no matter the history or fable.

I have them drink tea and eat dumplings,
as I hear them mumbling,
And sometimes a fight will break out.
"Put down the gun --
Hemingway - it's done."
Fitzgerald and Poe take his rounds.
At this lunch they're in tune,
and, while we men do
often insist on argument,
All thoughts and suggestions are brought into
question
in my imagination of patience.

In this rumbling mind-prison,
all face criticism;
Critics in listening to fellow critic, over each
niche obsession,
And, of course. I am
terrified to speak-
in the presence of such beards.
Hence, I watch instead,
with careful lend of ear.
My head, filling with lessons and personalities
-

Admittedly, some, I do poorly recreate.
but it matters not to me;

It matters only: what DOES resonate
in the matters they truly did speak.

They may argue of Justice --
perhaps over bottles of wine.
A structuralist may chime,
"If Justice is fair, then why is she blind?"
Oh, they would eat at it for hours.
Byron may note, "If a woman she be-,"
then turn to Dickinson, or poke at Shelley.
But Sappho and Yosano would then rise to
speak.
Sometimes the white beards make noise,
and I will not listen.
When they claim, "every man,"
I'll note who they're missing.

And I, in isolation, am set,
at Rizal, Buddha's and Dazai's left,
Behind them - yet still with much distance.
Bare faces may dictate my place,
or lack of my own greatness traced
to historical upheaval and resistance.
- But in some instance,
I arrived at their conclusions independently.

All tragic products of some broken nations,
their tragedy holds a true adoration.
For this exploration of tragedy

is my preferred taste in history.
No substance is found in fake royalty.
This imagination of mine holds more reality.
But, Jesus – this lunch can be messy.

So when I am frozen, unable to answer
some trivial, ethical or deep-moral matter,
Do not mistake me for spineless or lost,
when confronted with complex-context
content of nonsense.

Each question has infinite answers,
but so many lead me to none,
So please, imagine I answer a handful of
infinity,
and pack it all into one:
One messy answer for infinite's stead:
It's the best I can offer, I dread.
For I have too many masters - too many
disasters,
All having lunch in my head.

Reaching for the Fruit

Fellow man, why do you despise yourself?
You cry tears on your entanglement,
But where is your pride in your fulfilment?
Are we so desperate for destruction of us?
We only trust
we are made from dust.
and it seems it was only err we sought,
among battles fought, and not
the wonders we did find,
and wonders we created,
once banished from Eden – forever ill-fated.

The Angels should quake in Envy of us:
of our weakness and shame.
Our counted days of tear-shaped pain
slip to shine on blushing skin.
Is our beauty not our sin?
Why have we grown to hate it?
For we are weak, and we are wild
and we are terrified,
But without terror, courage hides.
and from our fall, we rise.

Heaven's Angels sing of Good,
and Hell hath Evil in its boast.

But humble earth with prided man
suffers time in both – alone, and ugly still.
Perhaps it is my ugliness,
and bruised hand holding scripture,
that seeks greater purpose, greater use,
for the Greater Picture – of our end.

When Michael flies down in triumph at
world's end,
to the cheers of rescued sinner,
his mighty sword tastes the dragon's scales,
measures the blood of it, running far thinner.
But see how he strikes down so easily?
Despite how his old fallen brother meets
his pained eyes in teary weak
reminiscence?
Before steel plunges down,
Will there be resistance?

Through wars and hatred, Man knows his sin:
He stands where the conquered once stood.
If Angels would conquer their own fallen
brother,
then Goodness should not be called good.
So I propose a newer plan
of Revelations – one of Man.
One where we, battered victims
to the cycle of endless violence,
are not forced to see re-cycled:

nothing less than vile ends.
And the Angels in Human weakness,
learn a truer strength in lesson:
To lend their Human arms
to enemies' redemption.

The God of some would strike me down
before my own mother,
if I try to call the good in another
of His own creation,
whom He has created Himself.
A creature – His son, created in Glory
whom now we must deem
unredeemable…

I am so much a sinner, I take pride in it:
But it is to love in firmer resolve.
The questions unsolved, I search in places
unsearched.
Does this mirror my oldest Mother,
reaching for fruit,
in search of You?
Will I find Truth? Does He want me to?
Must I cut my truest hopes
down to slivers?
Will He tell me to call Satan
Doomed and Damned Devil,
Or may I call him, "Lucifer"-
The Angel who fell?

Should God rejoice when redemption is done,
may it be in regaining His prodigal son,
and we, all tortured sinners, shamed
would call on fallen brother's name.
A simple hope – a holding hand.
But a hope is all
I can,
as Man.

www.ingramcontent.com/pod-product-compliance
Lightning Source LLC
Chambersburg PA
CBHW051734130826
49812CB00033B/859
9789357211819